# EUROPEAN HISTORY

## — 1848 to 1914 —
## Realism and Materialism

**William T. Walker, Ph.D.**
Chair, Department of Humanities and Associate Professor of History
Philadelphia College of Pharmacy and Science,
Philadelphia, Pennsylvania

Research and Education Association
61 Ethel Road West
Piscataway, New Jersey 08854

THE ESSENTIALS ®
OF EUROPEAN HISTORY
1848 to 1914:
Realism and Materialism

Printed in the United States of America

Library of Congress Catalog Card Number 97-65633

International Standard Book Number 0-87891-709-8

ESSENTIALS is a registered trademark of
Research & Education Association, Piscataway, New Jersey 08854

# What the "Essentials of History" Will Do for You

REA's "Essentials of History" series offers a new approach to the study of history that is different from what has been available previously. Each book in the series has been designed to steer a sensible middle course, by including neither too much nor too little information.

Compared with conventional history outlines, the "Essentials of History" offer far more detail, with fuller explanations and interpretations of historical events and developments. Compared with voluminous historical tomes and textbooks, the "Essentials of History" offer a far more concise, less ponderous overview of each of the periods they cover.

The "Essentials of History" are intended primarily to aid students in studying history, doing homework, writing papers and preparing for exams. The books are organized to provide quick access to information and explanations of the important events, dates, and persons of the period. The books can be used in conjunction with any text. They will save hours of study and preparation time while providing a firm grasp and insightful understanding of the subject matter.

Instructors too will find the "Essentials of History" useful. The books can assist in reviewing or modifying course outlines. They also can assist with preparation of exams, as well as serve as an efficient memory refresher.

In sum, the "Essentials of History" will prove to be handy reference sources at all times.

The authors of the series are respected experts in their fields. They present clear, well-reasoned explanations and interpretations of the complex political, social, cultural, economic and philosophical issues and developments which characterize each era.

In preparing these books REA has made every effort to assure their accuracy and maximum usefulness. We are confident that each book will prove enjoyable and valuable to its user.

Dr. Max Fogiel, Program Director

## *About the Author*

**William T. Walker** is currently the Chairman of the Department of Humanities and an associate professor of history at the Philadelphia College of Pharmacy and Science in Philadelphia, Pennsylvania, where he has served in this capacity since 1987. Previously, he held numerous teaching and administrative positions at Gwynedd-Mercy College at Gwynedd Valley, Pennsylvania, the University of South Carolina at Sumter, South Carolina, and Clemson University at Sumter, South Carolina.

Dr. Walker, the author of many scholarly articles, is a member of the American Historical Association, the Sixteenth Century Studies Conference, the Intellectual History Group, the Catholic Record Society (London), Phi Alpha Theta National History Honor Society, the North American Conference on British Studies, and the Society for Reformation Research. He has been the recipient of many awards and grants during his various tenures, and is an expert in Tudor-Stuart England, Modern Britain, and Europe since 1789.

# CONTENTS

# INTRODUCTION

Historians consider the period from the Revolutions of 1848 to the outbreak of the First World War in July – August 1914 to be an era which was characterized by the development of policies and strategies predicated upon a *realistic* (as opposed to romantic) assessment of conditions and objectives and by the growth and acceptance of *materialism* throughout Europe. The dramatic expansion of the industrial revolution coincided with the development of new nation-states within Europe and with the revival of European imperial activity overseas. In the more advanced societies, such as Britain, France, the Low Countries, and the Scandinavian states, this period also witnessed the extension of democracy in government and an apparent improvement in the general standard of living. While exhibiting the myriad of *progressive* characteristics, European states conducted their foreign policies along traditional lines; the relations of the European states with one another were rendered more complex and precarious with the impact of mass culture and the emergence of zealous patriotism. From the Revolutions of 1848 to the fateful summer of 1914, Europeans enjoyed an era of general peace and prosperity which was based on the assumption that European leaders had the capacity to identify and maintain the direction of European progress.

# CHAPTER 1

# EUROPE IN 1848

## 1.1   THE REVOLUTIONARY TRADITION

The era of reaction which had followed the collapse of the Napoleonic regime and the Congress of Vienna (1815) was followed by a wave of liberal and national agitation which was manifested in the Revolutions of 1820, 1825, and 1830.

The *liberals*, who tended to control the revolutionary agenda in Western Europe, desired constitutional government and the extension of individual freedoms – freedom of speech, press, and assembly. Liberal reforms and programs were advanced in the more economically advanced societies which had significant middle classes. In Central, Eastern, and Southern Europe, *nationalism* was the primary force for change. The advocates of nationalism sought to dismantle the traditional dynastic political controls which prohibited the formation of genuine nation-states. In addition to these factors, other reformers had succeeded in placing the need for social and economic improvement of the masses on the revolutionary platform; this was especially evident in France and England.

1

During the 1840s the movement toward revolutionary change was supported by four factors:

1) The failure of the existing regime to address the economic and social problems which accompanied the general economic collapse which occurred during the decade.

2) The regularity of significant food shortages in the major urban centers.

3) The increased popularity of the demands of the liberals and the nationalists.

4) The increasingly radical political, economic, and social proposals advanced by the *Utopian Socialists* (Charles Fourier, Robert Owen), the *Anarchists* (Pierre Proudhon), and the *Chartists* in England.

## 1.2 OUTBREAK AND DEVELOPMENT OF THE REVOLUTIONS OF 1848

### 1.2.1 *France*

The once liberal regime of King Louis Philippe (1830 – 1848) became increasingly conservative and oppressive under the leadership of Prime Minister Francois Guizot and the Chamber of Deputies. Guizot's opposition to reforms resulted in the further restriction of individual rights in general and the excessive use of censorship to silence critics of the regime.

The predominantly liberal opposition scheduled a banquet – which was a direct challenge to the regime – for the night of February 22, 1848. Guizot's government refused to sanction the banquet and, as a result, students and working class men

# THE REVOLUTIONS OF 1848

took to the streets and violence erupted. In an effort to eliminate further difficulty, Louis Philippe dismissed Guizot; however, on the evening of February 23, 1848, a conflict between
government troops and opponents of the regime occurred and
over fifty people were killed. Reports of the "massacre" spread
quickly and over a thousand barricades were erected. On February 24th, Louis Philippe attempted to develop a strategy
which would permit him to remain in power; but, by the end of
the day, he abdicated and fled to England.

A provisional government was established which represented the entire spectrum of opposition forces. The principal

tasks of the provisional government were (1) to serve as an interim authority, and (2) to arrange for the elections to a National Constituent Assembly. Among the representatives in the provisional government were Lamartine, a poet, and Louis Blanc, a socialist who was an advocate of National Workshops. During the spring of 1848 national workshops were established to resolve the problem of unemployment.

In April, French citizens voted for representatives to the National Constituent Assembly; the vote indicated that the nation supported the establishment of a republican government but that it was conservative in its economic and social philosophy. The Assembly convened in May and dissolved the national workshops; the result was the confrontation known as The June Days (June 23 – 27, 1848) during which French troops led by General Louis Eugene Cavaignac suppressed the radicals who wanted to maintain the workshops.

A new constitution was developed and accepted in October 1848. It established the Second French Republic which provided for a president and a single chamber assembly which would be elected on the basis of universal manhood suffrage; the president would serve a four-year term of office. The presidential election was held in December, 1848; Louis Napoleon, nephew of Napoleon I, easily defeated his rivals Cavaignac and Lamartine.

### 1.2.2 Prussia and the German States

News of the revolt in France resulted in rebellions in Prussia and other German states such as Baden, Bavaria, Hanover, and Saxony. The princes of the lesser states attempted to nullify the more strident demands of the revolutionaries by promising constitutions and appointing liberal ministers. However, King Frederick William IV of Prussia was adamant in his refusal to placate the revolutionaries; consequently, a violent revolution developed in Berlin.

On March 17, 1848, Frederick William IV relented and announced the following:

1) A Prussian assembly (*The Berlin Assembly*) would be convened in April, 1848.

2) A constitution would be developed.

3) Internal reforms would be instituted.

4) Prussia would assist in the development of a constitutional revitalization of the German Confederation.

*The Frankfurt Assembly*, which was a Pan-German assembly interested in the formulation of an integrated union of German states, convened in May 1848. During the next year, the group of liberals and nationalists developed a framework for a united Germany along the lines of the *Kleindeutsch* or Small Germany. This approach to German unification did not incorporate the Austrian Empire because of the great numbers of non-German peoples in that state; the advocates of the *Kleindeutsch* plan opposed the *Grossdeutsch* or Great Germany approach, which would have included Austria, because it violated the principle of national ethnic cohesion. In 1849, Frederick William IV received an offer to lead the new Germany. While interested in pursuing this opportunity, he declined because of the shift in the direction of the revolution; a reaction against the revolution had set in and most of the radical leaders fled the German states.

### 1.2.3 The Austrian Empire

Revolutionary activity broke out in Vienna on March 13, 1848. Within forty-eight hours, Prince Metternich, the symbol

5

of reaction throughout Europe, resigned as Foreign Minister. Ferdinand I, the Austrian Emperor, acquiesced and granted concessions including a pledge to support the development of a constitution and the extension of individual liberties.

The nationalist ambitions of the Hungarians were advanced by Louis Kossuth. On March 15, 1848, the Hungarian Diet declared a constitution which established a national assembly which was based on a limited franchise, specified individual freedoms, eliminated the remnants of the feudal order, and established an autonomous Hungary within the Austrian Empire. On March 31, 1848, the Austrian government accepted these substantive changes.

Czech nationalistic aspirations were manifested with the establishment of a *Bohemian Diet* in March. Its initial demands concerned universal manhood suffrage, guarantees of basic political and religious rights, and the parity of the Czech and German languages in education and government. On April 8th, Ferdinand I granted these concessions and rendered Bohemia an autonomous state. The further development of Czech nationalism was blurred by the emergence of the *Pan-Slavic Congress* (June 1848). The leaders of the Pan-Slavic Congress hoped to establish an autonomous government for Czechs, Slovaks, and other Slavs within the Austrian Empire.

*The April Decree* (April 11, 1848), which was issued by the Hapsburg government, pledged to eliminate the feudal services and duties which were still imposed on the peasants.

### 1.2.4  *Italy*

In the Italian peninsula revolutionary activity broke out in Milan in March 1848 and was directed primarily by nationalists who were interested in expelling the Austrians from Lombardy and Venetia. King Charles Albert of Sardinia and Piedmont capitalized on the revolution by declaring war on Austria. In central Italy, Pope Pius IX expressed support for a unified Italian state, and in the Kingdom of the Two Sicilies an isolated revolt in Palermo, which occurred earlier than the rebellion in Paris, resulted in the granting of a liberal constitution by the reactionary King Ferdinand II.

Throughout Italy the revolution emphasized the cause of Italian nationalism and the re-emergence of Italian pride through the *Risorgimento*. There was no evidence that the revolution was seriously concerned with the economic and social problems which confronted the Italian peasants.

Austrian Field Marshal Josef Graf Radetzky von Radetz withdrew the Austrian forces to the Quadrilateral, a series of fortresses on the Adige and Mincia. There Radetzky regrouped and, in July 1848, launched a counter-offensive which resulted in the resounding defeat of the Italian forces under Charles Albert at Custozza (July 25, 1848). In 1849 Charles Albert undertook another military initiative but was defeated by Radetzky at Novara (March 23, 1849); Charles Albert abdicated in favor of his son, Victor Emmanuel II.

## 1.3 THE FAILURE OF THE REVOLUTIONS, 1848 – 1849

By the summer of 1848, the revolutionary effort had been spent and the earlier gains of the late winter and spring had been reversed or challenged in many countries. The June Days in France coincided with the dissolution of the Pan-Slavic Congress in Prague by General Alfred Windischgratz. By October, Windischgratz had suppressed the revolution in Vienna, and Radetzky's armies were moving successfully against the Italians. In the fall and winter (1848 – 1849) the revolutions were stifled in France, Prussia, Austria, Italy, and other states.

The failure of the Revolutions of 1848 was due to several major factors:

1) The armed forces had remained loyal to the old leadership and demonstrated a willingness to assist in the suppression of the revolutions.

2) In Western Europe, the revolutionaries were appeased by liberal political reforms. In most instances, the majority of citizens in the West indicated that they were opposed to radical economic and social change.

3) In Central Europe, revolutions, which had been led by the middle class, did not express any interest in addressing social and economic problems. When the workers and students demanded social and economic revolution, the middle class became alienated from the revolution which they had led earlier; they desired only political change through the establishment of a constitutional process. This breach within the revolutionary camp was detected and exploited by the old regime.

4) In Eastern and Southern Europe, the nationalist revolutions lacked organization and, above all, the military capacity to resist the professional armies of the Austrian Empire.

By 1849 the revolutions had been suppressed or redirected. Only in France with the Second French Republic (1848 – 1852) and in Prussia (the Constitution of 1850) did some of the earlier gains endure.

# CHAPTER 2

# *REALPOLITIK* AND THE TRIUMPH OF NATIONALISM

## 2.1 CAVOUR AND THE UNIFICATION OF ITALY

After the collapse of the revolutionary movements of 1848, the leadership of Italian nationalism was transferred to Sardinian leaders (Victor Emmanuel II, Camillo de Cavour, and Giuseppe Garibaldi) who replaced the earlier leaders (Giuseppe Mazzini of the Young Italy movement, Charles Albert, the once liberal Pius IX, and V. Gioberti and the Neo-Guelf movement, which a unified Italian state centered on the Papacy). The new leadership did not entertain romantic illusions about the process of transforming Sardinia into a new Italian Kingdom; they were practitioners of the politics of realism, *realpolitik.*

Cavour (1810 – 1861) was a Sardinian who served as editor of *Il Risorgimento* which was a newspaper that argued that Sardinia should be the basis of a new Italy. Between 1852 and

1861 Cavour served as Victor Emmanuel II's Prime Minister. In that capacity Cavour transformed Sardinian society through the implementation of a series of liberal reforms which were designed to modernize the Sardinian state and attract the support of liberal states such as Great Britain and France. Among Cavour's reforms were the following:

1) The *Law on Convents* and the *Siccardi Law*, which were directed at curtailing the influence of the Roman Catholic Church;

2) the reform of the judicial system;

3) the full implementation of the *Statuto*, the Sardinian constitution which was modeled on the liberal French constitution of 1830; and

4) support for economic development projects such as port and highway construction.

In 1855, under Cavour's direction, Sardinia joined Britain and France in the Crimean War against Russia. At the Paris Peace Conference (1856), Cavour addressed the delegates on the need to eliminate the foreign (Austrian) presence in the Italian peninsula and attracted the attention and sympathy of the French Emperor, Napoleon III.

Cavour and Napoleon III met at Plombiérès (July 20, 1859); the *Plombières Agreement* stated that in the event that Sardinia went to war – presumably after being attacked or provoked – with Austria, that France would provide military assistance to Sardinia, and with victory, Sardinia would annex Lombardy, Venetia, Parma, Modena, and a part of the Papal states. Additionally, the remainder of Italy would be organized into an Italian Confederation under the direction of the Pope, France would receive Nice and Savoy, and the alliance would be finalized by a marriage between the two royal families. The Plombières Agreement was designed to bring about a war with Austria and to assist Sardinia in developing an expanded northern Italian kingdom. The concept of an Italian confederation under the Papacy was contributed by Napoleon III and demonstrates his lack of understanding about the nature of Italian political ambitions and values during this period.

After being provoked, the Austrians declared war on Sardinia in 1859. French forces intervened and the Austrians were defeated in the battles of Magenta (June 4) and Solferino (June 24). Napoleon III's support wavered for four reasons:

1) Prussia mobilized and expressed sympathy for Austria;

2) the outbreak of uncontrolled revolutions in several Northern Italian states;

3) the forcefulness of the new Austrian military efforts; and

4) the lack of public support in France for his involvement and the mounting criticism being advanced by the French Catholic Church, which opposed the war against Catholic Austria.

Napoleon III, without consulting Cavour, signed a secret peace (*The Truce of Villafranca*) on July 11, 1859. Sardinia received Lombardy but not Venetia; the other terms indicated that Sardinian influence would be restricted and that Austria would remain a power in Italian politics. The terms of Villafranca were clarified and finalized with the *Treaty of Zurich* (1859).

In 1860 Cavour arranged the annexation of Parma, Modena, Romagna, and Tuscany into Sardinia. These actions were recognized by the *Treaty of Turin* between Napoleon III and Victor Emmanuel II; Nice and Savoy were transferred to France. With these acquisitions, Cavour anticipated the need for a period of tranquility to incorporate these territories into Sardinia.

Giuseppe Garibaldi and his Red Shirts landed in Sicily (May 1860) and extended the nationalist activity to the south. Within three months, Sicily was taken and by September 7th, Garibaldi was in Naples and the Kingdom of the Two Sicilies had fallen under Sardinian influence. Cavour distrusted Garibaldi but Victor Emmanuel II encouraged him.

In February 1861, in Turin, Victor Emmanuel was declared King of Italy and presided over an Italian Parliament which represented the entire Italian peninsula with the exception of Venetia and the Patrimony of St. Peter (Rome). Cavour died in June 1861.

Venetia was incorporated into the Italian Kingdom in 1866 as a result of an alliance between Bismarck's Prussia and the Kingdom of Italy which preceded the German Civil War between Austria and Prussia. In return for opening a southern front against Austria, Prussia, upon its victory, arranged for Venetia to be transferred to Italy.

Bismarck was again instrumental in the acquisition of Rome into the Italian Kingdom in 1870. In 1870 the Franco-Prussian War broke out and the French garrison, which had been in Rome providing protection for the Pope, was withdrawn to serve on the front against Prussia. Italian troops seized Rome and, in 1871, as a result of a plebiscite, Rome became the capital of the Kingdom of Italy.

# THE UNIFICATION OF ITALY

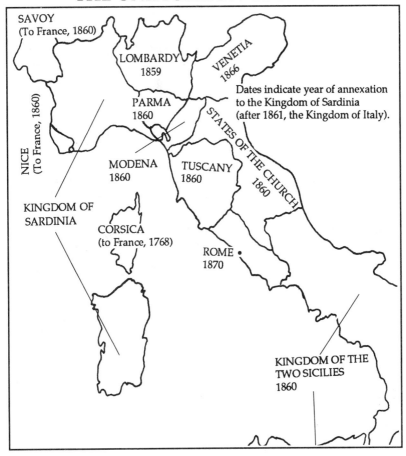

SAVOY
(To France, 1860)

LOMBARDY
1859

VENETIA
1866

Dates indicate year of annexation
to the Kingdom of Sardinia
(after 1861, the Kingdom of Italy).

NICE
(To France, 1860)

PARMA
1860

STATES OF THE CHURCH
1860

MODENA
1860

TUSCANY
1860

KINGDOM OF
SARDINIA

CORSICA
(to France, 1768)

ROME •
1870

KINGDOM OF THE
TWO SICILIES
1860

## 2.2 BISMARCK AND THE UNIFICATION OF GERMANY

During the period after 1815 Prussia emerged as an alternative to a Hapsburg-based Germany. During the early nineteenth century, Germany was politically decentralized and consisted of dozens of independent states. This multi-state situation had been in place for centuries and had been sanctioned by the Peace of Westphalia in 1648. Prussia had absorbed many of the

13

smaller states during the eighteenth and early nineteenth centuries.

*Otto von Bismarck* (1810 – 1898) entered the diplomatic service of William I as the Revolutions of 1848 were being suppressed. By the early 1860s Bismarck had emerged as the principal adviser and minister to the King. Bismarck was an advocate of a Prussian-based (Hohenzollern) Germany. During the 1850s and 1860s Bismarck supported a series of military reforms which improved the Prussian army. In 1863 Bismarck joined the Russians in suppressing a Polish rebellion; this enterprise resulted in improved Russian-Prussian relations.

In 1863, the *Schleswig-Holstein* crisis broke. These provinces, which were occupied by Germans, were under the personal rule of Christian IX of Denmark. The Danish government advanced a new constitution which specified that Schleswig and Holstein would be annexed into Denmark. German reaction was predictable and Bismarck arranged for a joint Austro-Prussian military action. Denmark was defeated and agreed (*Treaty of Vienna*, 1864) to give up the provinces. Schleswig and Holstein were to be jointly administered by the victors, Austria and Prussia.

Questions of jurisdiction provided the rationale for estranged relations between Austria and Prussia. In 1865 a temporary settlement was reached in the *Gastein Convention*, which stated that Prussia would administer Schleswig and Austria would manage Holstein. During 1865 and 1866, Bismarck made diplomatic preparations for the forthcoming struggle with Austria. Italy, France, and Russia would not interfere, and Great Britain was not expected to involve itself in a Central European war.

*The German Civil War* (also known as *The Seven Weeks' War*) was devastating to Austria. The humiliating defeat at Koniggratz (July 4, 1866) demonstrated the ineptitude of the Austrian forces when confronted by the Prussian army led by General von Moltke. Within two months, Austria had to agree to the peace terms which were drawn up at Nikolsburg and finalized by the *Peace of Prague* (August 1866). There were three principal terms:

1) Austria would not be part of any new German state. The *Kleindeutsch* plan had prevailed over the *Grossdeutsch* plan.

2) Venetia would be ceded to Italy.

3) Austria would pay an indemnity to Prussia.

In the next year, 1867, the *North German Confederation* was established by Bismarck. It was designed to facilitate the movement toward a unified German state and included all the German states except Baden, Württemberg, Bavaria, and Saxony; the King of Prussia served as President of the Confederation.

In 1870, the deteriorating relations between France and Germany became critical over the *Ems Dispatch*. William I, while vacationing at Ems, was approached by representatives of the French government who requested a Prussian pledge not to interfere on the issue of the vacant Spanish throne. William I refused to give such a pledge and informed Bismarck of these developments through a telegram from Ems.

Bismarck exploited the situation by initiating a propaganda campaign against the French. Subsequently, France declared war and the Franco-Prussian War (1870 – 1871) commenced. Prussian victories at Sedan and Metz proved decisive; Napoleon III and his leading general, Marshal MacMahon, were captured. Paris continued to resist but fell to the Prussians in

15

# THE UNIFICATION OF GERMANY

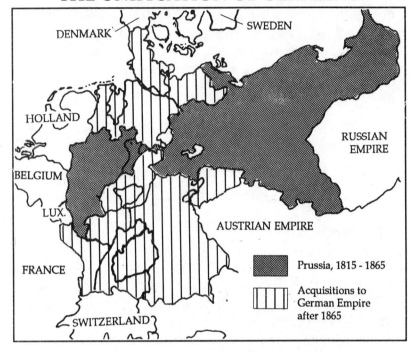

January 1871. The *Treaty of Frankfurt* (May, 1871) concluded the war and resulted in France ceding Alsace-Lorraine to Germany and a German occupation until an indemnity was paid.

The German Empire was proclaimed on January 18, 1871 with William I becoming the Emperor of Germany. Bismarck became the Imperial Chancellor. Bavaria, Baden, Württemberg, and Saxony were incorporated into the new Germany.

# CHAPTER 3

# INTER-EUROPEAN RELATIONS, 1848 – 1878

## 3.1 INTRODUCTION

Since the Napoleonic era the peace in Europe had been sustained because of the memories of the devastation and the disruption caused by the wars of the French Revolution and Napoleonic Age; the primary structure which maintained the peace was the *Concert System*. The Concert of Europe was a rather loose and ill-defined understanding among the European nations that they would join together to resolve problems which threatened the status quo; it was believed that joint action would be undertaken to prohibit any drastic alteration in the European system or balance of power. The credibility of the Concert of Europe was undermined by the failure of the powers to cooperate during the revolution of 1848 and 1849. Between 1848 and 1878 the peace among the European powers was interrupted by the Crimean War (1854 – 56) and challenged by the crisis centered on the Russo-Turkish War of 1877 – 78.

## 3.2  THE CRIMEAN WAR

The origins of the Crimean War are to be found in the dispute between two differing groups of Christians (and their protectors) over privileges in the *Holy Land*. During the nineteenth century Palestine was part of the Ottoman Turkish Empire. In 1852, the Turks negotiated an agreement with the French to provide enclaves in the Holy Land to Roman Catholic religious orders; this arrangement appeared to jeopardize already existing agreements which provided access to Greek Orthodox religious orders. Czar Nicholas, unaware of the impact of his action, ordered Russian troops to occupy several Danubian principalities; his strategy was to withdraw from these areas once the Turks agreed to clarify and guarantee the rights of the Greek Orthodox orders. The role of Britain in this developing crisis was critical; Nicholas mistakenly was convinced that the British Prime Minister, Lord Aberdeen, would be sympathetic to the Russian policy. Aberdeen, who headed a coalition cabinet, sought to use the Concert of Europe system to settle the question. However, Lord Palmerston, the Home Secretary, supported the Turks; he was suspicious of Russian intervention in the region. Consequently, misunderstandings about Britain's policy developed. In October, 1853, the Turks demanded that the Russians withdraw from the occupied principalities; the Russians failed to respond and the Turks declared war. In February, 1854 Nicholas advanced a draft for a settlement of the Russo-Turkish War; it was rejected and Great Britain and France joined the Ottoman Turks and declared war on Russia.

With the exception of some naval encounters in the Gulf of Finland off the Aaland Islands, this war was conducted on the Crimean peninsula in the Black Sea. In September, 1854, over 50,000 British and French troops landed in the Crimea, determined to take the Russian port city of Sebastopol. While this

18

war has been remembered for the work of Florence Nighten-gale and the "Charge of the Light Brigade", it was a conflict in which there were more casualties from disease and the weather than from combat. In December 1854, Austria, with great reluctance, became a co-signatory of the *Four Points of Vienna* which was a statement of British and French war aims. The Four Points specified that (1) Russia should renounce any claims to the occupied principalities, (2) the 1841 Straits Convention would be revised, (3) navigation in the mouth of the Danube River (on the Black Sea) should be internationalized, and (4) Russia should withdraw any claim to having a 'special' protective role for Greek Orthodox residents in the Ottoman Empire. In 1855, Piedmont joined Britain and France in the war. In March 1855 Czar Nicholas died and was succeeded by Alexander II who was opposed to continuing the war. In December 1855, the Austrians, under excessive pressure from the British, French, and Piedmontese, sent an ultimatum to Russia in which they threatened to renounce their neutrality. In response Alexander II indicated that he would accept the Four Points.

Representatives of the belligerents convened in Paris between February and April 1856. The resulting *Peace of Paris* had the following major provisions:

1) Russia had to

- acknowledge international commissions which were to regulate maritime traffic on the Danube,

- recognize Turkish control of the mouth of the Danube,

- renounce all claims to the Danubian Principalities of

Moldavia and Wallachia (this later led to the establishment of Rumania),

- agree not to fortify the Aaland Islands,

- renounce its previously espoused position of protector of the Greek Orthodox residents of the Ottoman Empire, and

- return all occupied territories to the Ottoman Empire.

2) The Straits Convention of 1841 was revised through the neutralization of the Black Sea.

3) The *Declaration of Paris* specified the rules which would regulate commerce during periods of war.

4) The independence and integrity of the Ottoman Empire were recognized and guaranteed by the signatories.

## 3.3 THE EASTERN QUESTION TO THE CONGRESS OF BERLIN

Another challenge to the Concert of Europe developed in the 1870s with a seemingly endless number of Balkan crises. Once again, the conflict initially involved Russia and Ottoman Turks but it quickly became a conflict with Britain and Russia serving as the principal protagonists. British concerns over Russian ambitions in the Balkans reached a critical level in 1877 when Russia went to war with the Turks.

*The Causes.* In 1876, the Turkish forces under the leadership of Osman Pasha soundly defeated the Serbian armies. Serbia requested assistance from the great powers and, as a consequence of the political pressures exercised by the great powers, the Turks agreed to participate in a conference in Constantinople; the meeting resulted in a draft agreement between the Serbs and the Turks. However, Britain quietly advised the Sultan, Abdul Hamid II, to scuttle the agreement, which he did. In June 1877 Russia dispatched forces across the Danube. During the next month, Osman Pasha took up a defensive position in Plevna. During the period of the siege, sympathy in the west shifted toward the Turks, and Britain and Austria became alarmed over the extent of Russian influence in the region. In March 1878, the Russians and the Turks signed the *Peace of San Stephano*; implementation of its provisions would have resulted in Russian hegemony in the Balkans and dramatically altered the balance of power in the eastern Mediterranean. Specifically it provided for the following:

1) the establishment of a large Bulgarian state which would be under Russian influence;

2) the transfer of Dobrudja, Kars, Ardahan, Bayazid, and Batum to Russia;

3) expanded Serbia and Montenegro; and

4) the establishment of an autonomous Bosnia-Herzegovina which would be under Russian control.

Britain, under the leadership of Prime Minister Benjamin Disraeli, denounced the San Stephano Accord, dispatched a naval squadron to Turkish waters, and demanded that the San Stephano agreement be scrapped. The German Chancellor, Otto von Bismarck, intervened and offered his services as mediator.

*The Congress of Berlin.* The delegates of the major pow-

21

ers convened in June and July 1878 to negotiate a settlement. Prior to the meeting, Disraeli had concluded a series of secret arrangements with Austria, Russia and Turkey. The combined impact of these accommodations was to restrict Russian expansion in the region, reaffirm the independence of Turkey, and maintain British control of the Mediterranean. The specific terms of the *Treaty of Berlin* resulted in the following:

1) Recognition of Rumania, Serbia and Montenegro as independent states;

2) the establishment of the autonomous principality of Bulgaria,

3) Austrian acquisition of Bosnia and Herzegovina; and

4) the transfer of Cyprus to Great Britain.

The Russians, who had won the war against Turkey and had imposed the harsh terms of the San Stephano Treaty, found that they left the conference with very little (Kars, Batum, etc.) for their effort. Although Disraeli was the primary agent of this anti-Russian settlement, the Russians blamed Bismarck for their dismal results. Their hostility toward Germany led Bismarck (1879) to embark upon a new system of alliances which transformed European diplomacy and rendered any additional efforts of the Concert of Europe futile.

# CHAPTER 4

# CAPITALISM AND THE EMERGENCE OF THE NEW LEFT, 1848 – 1914

## 4.1 ECONOMIC DEVELOPMENTS: THE NEW INDUSTRIAL ORDER

During the nineteenth century, Europe experienced the full impact of the Industrial Revolution. The new economic order not only altered the working lives of most Europeans, but also impacted on the very fiber of European culture. The shifts in demography (see Appendix) were revolutionary; the process of urbanization was irreversible and the transformation of European values and lifestyle were dramatic. The Industrial Revolution resulted in improving aspects of the physical lives of a greater number of Europeans; at the same time, it led to a factory system with undesirable working and living conditions and the abuses of child labor. While the advantages of industrialism were evident, the disadvantages were more subtle; the industrial working class was more vulnerable than the agrarian peasants because of the fragile nature of the industrial economy. This new economy was based on a dependent system which involved (1) the availability of raw materials, (2) an adequate labor supply, and (3) a distribution system which successfully marketed the products; the distribution system was in itself dependent upon a satisfactory availability of money throughout the economic system. If any one of these requirements was impeded or absent, the industrial work force could be confronted with unemployment and poverty. The industrial system was based fundamentally in developing capitalism which itself was essentially grounded in an appreciation of material culture. The standard of living, neo-mercantilist attitudes towards national power, and the goal of accumulation of wealth were manifestations of this materialism.

As the century progressed, the inequities of the system became increasingly evident. Trade-unionism and socialist political parties emerged which attempted to address these problems and improve the lives of the working class. In most of these expressions of discontent, the influences of Utopian Socialism or Marxism were evident and can be detected readily. Socialism was steeped in economic materialism which had emerged in the eighteenth century and came to dominate the nineteenth and twentieth centuries. Economics was a component in the rise of scientism; by its very nature, it advanced the values of material culture.

## 4.2   MARX AND SCIENTIFIC SOCIALISM

During the period from 1815 to 1848, *Utopian Socialists*, such as Robert Owen, Saint Simon, and Charles Fourier advocated the establishment of a political-economic system which was based on romantic concepts of the ideal society. The failure of the Revolutions of 1848 and 1849 discredited the Utopian Socialists, and the new "Scientific Socialism" advanced by

Karl Marx (1818 – 1883) became the primary ideology of protest and revolution. Marx, a German philosopher, developed a communist philosophic system which was founded on the inherent goodness of man; this Rousseau-influenced position argued that men were basically good but had been corrupted by the artificial institutions (states, churches, etc.) from which they had evolved. Marx stated that the history of humanity was the history of class struggle and that the process of the struggle (the dialectic) would continue until a classless society was realized; the Marxian dialectic was driven by the dynamics of materialism. Further, he contended that the age of the bourgeois domination of the working class was the most severe and oppressive phase of the struggle. The proletariat, or the industrial working class, needed to be educated and led towards a violent revolution which would destroy the institutions which perpetuated the struggle and the suppression of the majority. After the revolution, the people would experience the dictatorship of the proletariat during which the Communist Party would provide leadership. Marx advanced these concepts in a series of tracts and books including *The Communist Manifesto* (1848), *Critique of Political Economy* (1859), and *Capital* (1863 – 64). In most instances, his arguments were put forth in scientific form; Marx accumulated extensive data and developed a persuasive rhetorical style. In the 1860s Marxism was being accepted by many reformers. Marx lived most of his adult life in London where he died in 1883.

## 4.3   THE ANARCHISTS

Anarchism emerged in the early nineteenth century as a consequence of the industrial revolution. Its early proponents, William Godwin (1756 – 1836) and Pierre Proudhon (1809 – 65) argued that anarchism, a situation where there would be no property or authority, would be attained through enlightened individualism. Proudhon, in *What is Property* (1840), stated that anarchism would be achieved through education and without violence. After the revolutions of 1848 and 1849, Michael Bakunin, a Russian, stated that violent, terrorist actions were necessary to move the people to revolt against their oppressors; anarchism has been associated with violence since Bakunin's time. A variation of anarchism, *syndicalism*, was developed by Georges Sorel in France. Syndicalism, sometimes referred to as anarcho-syndicalism, involved direct economic actions in order to control industries. The strike and industrial sabotage were employed frequently by the syndicalists. Syndicalist influence was restricted to France, Spain (*Confederacion Nacional del Trabajo*, an organization of several syndicalist unions), and Italy (Filippo Corridoni and the young Benito Mussolini).

## 4.4 THE REVISIONIST MOVEMENT

A reconsideration of Marxism commenced before Marx's death in 1883. In that year a group of British leftists organized themselves into the *Fabian Society* and declared that while they were sympathetic to Marxism – indeed, they considered themselves Marxists – they differed from the orthodoxy on two major points: (1) they did not accept the inevitability of revolution in order to bring about a socialist, i.e. communist society; democratic societies possessed the mechanisms which would lead to the gradual evolution of socialism; (2) the Fabians did not accept the Marxist interpretation of contemporary history; they contended the historical processes endured and were difficult to redirect and reform, while Marxists tended to accept the notion that world revolution was imminent. Sidney and Beatrice Webb, George Bernard Shaw, Keir Hardie, and several others joined in forming the Fabian Society. Later it would split over the Boer War but its members would serve in every Labor ministry.

In Germany the *Social Democratic Party (SDP)* had

been established along the lines of Marxist orthodoxy. In the 1890s, Edward Bernstein (1850 – 1932), who was influenced by the Fabians, redirected the efforts and platform of the SDP toward the revisionist position. Within a few years, the SDP extended its credibility and support to acquire a dominant position in the Reichstag.

The French Socialist Jean Jaures (1859 – 1914) led his group to revisionism; their moderation led to increasing their seats in the Chamber of Deputies and in developing acceptance for their criticisms and proposals during the tumultuous years of the Dreyfus Affair.

While orthodox Marxists (Lenin) denounced the revisionist movement, the majority of socialists in 1914 were revisionists who were willing to use the democratic process to bring about their goals.

# CHAPTER 5

# BRITAIN AND FRANCE

During the second half of the nineteenth century, Britain and France enjoyed considerable economic prosperity, experienced periods of jingoistic nationalism, and were confronted with demands for expanding democracy. Great Britain, under the leadership of Lord Palmerston, William Gladstone and Benjamin Disraeli, represented a dichotomy of values and political agendas. On one hand, Britain led Europe into an age of revitalized imperialism and almost unbridled capitalism; on the other hand, Gladstone and the Liberal Party advocated democratic reforms, an anti-imperialist stance, and a program to eliminate or restrict unacceptable working and social conditions. In France, the evolution of a more democratic political order was questioned by the collapse of the Second French Republic and the development of the Second Empire. However, in 1871, the Third Republic was established and the French moved closer to realizing democracy.

## 5.1   THE AGE OF PALMERSTON

During the period from 1850 to 1865, Lord Palmerston was the dominant political power in Great Britain. Palmerston served in a range of positions including Foreign Secretary, Home Secretary, and Prime Minister. In foreign affairs Palmerston was preoccupied with colonial problems such as the Indian Muting of 1857, troubles in China, and British interests in the American Civil War; Palmerston tended to express little interest in domestic affairs. This period witnessed the realignment of political parties within British politico; the Tory Party was transformed into the Conservative Party under Disreali and the Whig Party became the Liberty Party with Gladstone serving as its new leader. It should be noted that John Bright, a manufacturer, anti-corn law advocate, and leader of the Manchester School, contributed significantly to the development of the Liberal Party. These changes in party organization involved more than appellations. The new structure more clearly represented distinct ideological positions on many substantive issues. The new political structure was facilitated by Palmerston's (the Whig) lack of interest in domestic issues and Lord Derby's (the Tory leader) indifference to political issues; he was preoccupied with his study of the classics and with horse racing.

Until the 1850s the British East India Company managed India for the British government. During this decade a new rifle, the Enfield, was introduced. The procedure for loading the Enfield required that the covering for the cartridges be removed by the teeth prior to inserting them in the rifle. Rumors circulated that the covering was a grease made from the fat of cows and swine; naturally, these rumors alarmed the Hindu and Muslim troops. Troops mutinied in Calcutta in 1857 and within a few months over a third of India was in the hands of rebels and Europeans were being killed. A British led force of about 3,000 troops under Sir Hugh Rose suppressed the mutiny which lacked cohesion in its aims, organization, and leadership. By January 1858, Britain had re-established its control of India; the East India Company was dissolved and replaced by the direct authority of London.

During the 1850s and 1860s Palmerston sought to clarify British commercial access to China. In 1858, with the support of French troops, the British army took the Taka Forts on the Peiko River and, in 1860, captured Peking. As a result, China agreed to open Tientsin and other ports to the European powers.

The American Civil War (1861 – 65) curtailed the supply of unprocessed cotton to British mills. The British economy was affected adversely and significant unemployment and factory closings resulted. The American war also led to a discussion within Britain on the fundamental issues of liberty, slavery, and democracy. A crisis between Britain and the United States developed over the *Trent Affair* (1861) during which a British ship was boarded by American sailors. In the end, the British government and people supported the Union cause because of ideological considerations; even in the areas affected by the shortage of cotton, there was general support for the North.

## 5.2 DISRAELI, GLADSTONE, AND THE ERA OF DEMOCRATIC REFORMS

In 1865 Palmerston died and during the next two decades significant domestic developments occured which expanded democracy in Great Britain. The dominant leaders of this period were William Gladstone (1809 – 1898) and Benjamin Disraeli (1804 – 1881). Gladstone, who was initially a Conservative, emerged as a severe critic of the Corn Laws and, as a budgetary expert, became Chancellor of the Exchequer under Palmerston. As the leader of the Liberal Party (to 1895), Gladstone supported Irish Home Rule, fiscal responsibility, free trade, and the extension of democratic principles; he was opposed to imperialism, the involvement of Britain in European affairs, and the further centralization of the British government.

Disraeli argued for an aggressive foreign policy, the expansion of the British Empire, and, after opposing democratic reforms, the extension of the franchise.

After defeating Gladstone's effort to extend the vote in 1866, Disraeli advanced the *Reform Bill of 1867*. This bill, which expanded on the *Reform Bill of 1832*, was enacted and specified two reforms:

1) There would be a *redistribution* (similar to reapportionment) of seats which would provide a more equitable representation in the House of Commons; the industrial cities and boroughs gained seats at the expense of some depopulated areas in the north and west.

2) The *right to vote* was extended to include (1) all adult male citizens of boroughs who paid £10 or more rent annually, and (2) all adult male citizens of the counties who were £12 tenants or £5 leaseholders.

The consequence of this act was that almost all men over 21 years in age who resided in urban centers were granted the right to vote. In 1868, the newly extended electorate provided the Liberals with a victory and Gladstone commenced his first of four terms as Prime Minister.

Gladstone's first ministry (1868 – 1874) was characterized by a wave of domestic legislation which reflected the movement toward democracy. Among the measures which were enacted were five acts:

1) *The Ballot Act* (1872) which provided for the secret ballot; this act realized a major Chartist demand of the 1830s;

2) *Civil Services Reform* (1870) which introduced the sys-

tem of competitive examination for government positions,

3) *The Education Act* (1870) which established a system of school districts throughout the country, and provided assistance in the organization of school boards, and for the establishment of schools in poverty stricken regions; free elementary education in Britain would not be realized until 1891,

4) *The Land Act* (1870) was an attempt to resolve economic and social inequities in Ireland. However, it did not succeed in providing Irish tenants with reasonable safeguards against arbitrary eviction or the imposition of drastic increases in rent, and

5) *The University Act* (1870) eliminated the use of religious tests which provided a quota of seats in universities for members of the Anglican church.

Between 1874 and 1880 Disraeli served as Prime Minister, and while he was deeply concerned with foreign difficulties, he did succeed in developing the notion of *Tory Democracy* which was directed at domestic issues. Tory Democracy represented Disreali's views on how the Conservative Party would support necessary domestic action on behalf of the common good. In 1875, through Disraeli's support, the following measures were passed:

1) Laws which lessened the regulation of trade unions;

2) *Food and Drug Act* which regulated the sale of these items;

3) *Public Health Act* which specified government re-

quirements and standards for sanitation;

4) *The Artisan's Dwelling Act.*

While a few Conservatives, such as Lord Randolph Churchill, attempted to extend the progress of Tory Democracy and to incorporate it permamently within the Conservative program, most of the Conservative Party abandoned this approach after Disraeli's death in 1881.

During his remaining ministries (1880 – 85, 1886, and 1892 – 95), Gladstone was preoccupied with Ireland. However, a further extension of the franchise occurred in 1884 with the passage of the *Representation of the People Act* which granted the right to vote to adult males in the counties on the same basis as in the boroughs. In 1885 another redistribution of seats in the House of Commons was approved on the ratio of one seat for every 50,000 citizens.

# 5.3   THE SECOND FRENCH REPUBLIC AND THE SECOND EMPIRE

Louis Napoleon became the President of the Second French Republic in December 1848. It was evident that he was not committed to the Republic; in May 1849, elections for the Legislative Assembly clearly indicated that the people were not bound to its continuance either. In this election, the Conservatives and Monarchists scored significant gains; the republicans and radicals lost power in the Assembly. During the three year life of the Second Republic, Louis Napoleon demonstrated his skills as a gifted politican through the manipulation of the various factions in French politics. His deployment of troops in Italy to rescue and restore Pope Pius IX was condemned by the republicans but strongly supported by the monarchists and moderates. As a consequence of the French military intervention, a French garrison under General Oudinot was stationed in Rome until the fall of 1870 when it was recalled during the Franco-Prussian War.

Louis Napoleon initiated a policy which minimized the importance of the Legislative Assembly, capitalized on the developing Napoleonic Legend, and courted the support of the army, the Catholic Church, and a range of conservative political groups. The Falloux Law returned control of education to the church. Further, Louis Napoleon was confronted with Article 45 of the constitution which stipulated that the president was limited to one four-year term; he had no intention of relinquishing power. With the assistance of a core of dedicated supporters, Louis Napoleon arranged for a *coup d'etat* on the night of December 1 – 2, 1851. The Second Republic fell and was soon replaced by the Second French Empire.

Louis Napoleon drafted a new constitution which resulted in a highly centralized government centered around himself. He was to have a ten year term, power to declare war, to lead the armed forces, to conduct foreign policy, and to initiate and pronounce all laws; the new Legislative Assembly would be under the control of the president. On December 2, 1852, he announced that he was Napoleon III, Emperor of the French.

The domestic history of the Second Empire is divided into two periods: 1851 to 1860, during which Napoleon III's control was direct and authoritarian, and 1860 to 1870, the decade of the *Liberal Empire*, during which the regime was liberalized through a series of reforms. During the Second Empire, living conditions in France generally improved. The government instituted agreements and actions which stimulated the movement toward free trade (*Cobden-Chevalier Treaty* of 1860), improved the efficiency of the French economic system (*Credit Mobilier and the Credit Focier*, both established in 1852), and

34

conducted major public works programs in French cities with the assistance of such talented leaders as Baron Haussmann, the prefect of the Seine. Even though many artists and scholars (Victor Hugo, Jules Michelet, and Gustav Flaubert) were censored and, on occasion, prosecuted for their works, the artistic and scholarly achievements of the Second Empire were impressive. While Flaubert and Baudelaire, and in music, Jacques Offenbach, were most productive during these decades, younger artists, such as Renoir, Manet, and Cezanne began their careers and were influenced by the culture of the Second Empire. The progressive liberalization of the government during the 1860s resulted in extending the powers of the Legislative Assembly, restricting church control over secondary education, and permitting the development of trade unions. In large part, this liberalization was designed to divert criticism from Napoleon III's unsuccessful foreign policy. French involvement in Algeria, the Crimean War, the process of Italian unification, the establishment of colonial presences in Senegal, Somaliland, and Indo-China (Laos, Cambodia, and Viet Nam), and the ill-fated Mexican adventure (the short-lived rule of Maximilian), resulted in increased criticism of Napoleon III and his authority. The Second Empire collapsed after the capture of Napoleon III during the Franco-Prussian War (1870 – 71). After a regrettable Parisian experience with a communist type of government, the Third French Republic was established; it would survive until 1940.

# CHAPTER 6

# EASTERN EUROPE,
# 1848 – 1914

## 6.1   IMPERIAL RUSSIA

The autocracy of Nicholas I's regime was not threatened by the revolutionary movements of 1848. The consequences of the European revolutionary experience of 1848 to 1849 reinforced the conservative ideology which was the basis of the Romanov regime. In 1848 and 1849, Russian troops suppressed disorganized Polish attempts to reassert Polish nationalism.

Russian involvement in the Crimean war (see Chapter 3) met with defeat. France, Britain, and Piedmont emerged as the victors in this conflict; Russian ambitions in the eastern Mediterranean had been thwarted by a coalition of western European states. In 1855 Nicholas I died and was succeeded by Alexander II (1855 – 1881) who feared the forces of change and introduced reforms in order to remain in power.

Fearing the transformation of Russian society from below, Alexander II instituted a series of reforms which contributed to altering the nature of the social contract in Russia. With the regime in disarray after defeat in the Crimean War, Alexander II, in March 1856, indicated that Russian serfdom had to be eliminated. After several years of formulating the process for its elimination, Alexander II pronounced in 1861 that serfdom was abolished. Further, he issued the following reforms:

1) The serf (peasant) would no longer be dependent upon the lord;

2) all people were to have freedom of movement and were free to change their means of livelihood; and

3) the serf (peasant) could enter into contracts and could own property.

In fact, the lives of most peasants were not affected by these reforms. Most peasants lived in local communes which regulated the lives of their members; thus, the requirements of commune life nullified the reforms of Alexander II. Another significant development was the creation of the *zemstvos,* which were assemblies which administered the local areas; through the *zemstvos* the Russian rural nobility retained control over local politics. Finally, Alexander II reformed the Russian judiciary system; the new judiciary was to be based upon such enlightened notions as jury trial, the abolition of arbitrary judicial processes, and the equality of all before the law. In fact, the only substantive change was the improvement in the efficiency of the Russian judiciary; however, the reforms did lead to expectations which were later realized.

The reforms of Alexander II did not resolve the problems of Russia. During the 1860s and 1870s criticism of the regime mounted. Moderates called for Russia to proceed along Western lines in a controlled manner in addressing political and economic problems; radicals argued that the overthrow of the system was the only recourse to the problems which confronted the Russian people. Quite naturally, Alexander II and other members of the power structure maintained that Russia would solve its own problems within the existing structure and without external intervention. The economic problems which plagued Russia were staggering. Under the three-field system which was utilized, one third of Russian agricultural land was not being used; the population was increasing dramatically but food protection was not keeping pace. Peasants were allowed to buy land and to live outside of the communes; however, even with the establishment of the *Peasants Land Bank* (1883), most peasants were unable to take advantage of this opportunity to become property owners. During years of great hardship, the government did intervene with emergency measures which temporarily reduced, deferred, or suspended taxes and/or payments.

While Russian agriculture appeared to have no direction nor to have experienced any real growth during this period, Russian industry, particularly in textiles and metallurgy, did develop. Between 1870 and 1900, as the result of French loans, the Russian railroad network was expanded significantly. In large part, the expansion of Russian industry resulted from direct governmental intervention. In addition to constructing railroads, the government subsidized industrial development through a protective tariff and by awarding major contracts to emerging industries. From 1892 to 1903 Count S. Y. Witte served as Minister of Finance. As a result of his efforts to stimulate the economy, Russian industry prospered during most of the 1890s. During this same period the government consistently suppressed the development of organized labor. In 1899 a depression broke and the gains of the 1890s quickly were replaced by the increased unemployment and industrial shutdowns; this very difficult situation was aggravated by the outbreak of the Russo-Japanese war in 1904.

The last years of the reign of Alexander II witnessed increased political opposition which was manifested in demands for reforms from an ever more hostile group of intellectuals, the emergence of a Russian populist movement, and attempts to assassinate the Czar. Some of the demands for extending reforms came from within the government from such dedicated and talented ministers as D. A. Miliutin, a Minister of War, who reorganized the Russian military system during the 1870s. However, reactionary ministers such as Count Dimitri Tolstoy, Minister of Education, did much to discredit any progressive policies emanating from the regime; Tolstoy repudiated academic freedom and advanced an anti-scientism bias. As the regime matured, greater importance was placed on traditional values. This attitude developed at the same time that *nihilism*, which rejected romantic illusions of the past in favor of a rugged realism, was being advanced by such writers as Ivan Turgenev in his *Fathers and Sons*.

The notion of the inevitability and desirability of a social and economic revolution was promoted through the Russian populist movement; originally, the populists were interested in an agrarian utopian order in which the lives of all peasants would be transformed into an idyllic state. The populists had no national base of support; government persecution of the populist resulted in the radicalization of the movement. In the late 1870s and early 1880s, leaders such as Andrei Zheleabov and Sophie Perovsky became obsessed with the need to assassinate Alexander II. In March, 1881, he was killed in St. Petersburg when his carriage was bombed; he was succeeded by Alexander III (1881 – 1894) who advocated a national policy based on "Orthodoxy, Autocracy, and Nationalism." Alexander III selected as his primary aides conservatives such as Count Dimitri Tolstoy, now Minister of the Interior, Count Delianov, Minister of Education, and Constantine Pobedonostev, who headed the Russian Orthodox Church. Alexander III died in

1894 and was succeeded by the last of the Romanovs to hold power, Nicholas II (1894 – 1917). Nicholas II displayed his lack of intelligence, wit, and political acumen, and the absence of a firm will throughout his reign. From assertive ministers to his wife, Alexandra, to Rasputin, Nicholas tended to come under the influence of stronger personalities. The crisis confronting Imperial Russia required extraordinarily effective and cohesive leadership; with Nicholas II, the situation became more severe and, in the end, unacceptable.

The opposition to the Czarist government became more focused and thus, more threatening, with the emergence of the **Russian Social Democrats** and the **Russian Social Revolutionaries**; both groups were Marxist. Vladimir Ilyich Ulyanov, also known as Lenin, became the leader of the Bolsheviks, a splinter group of the Social Democrats. Until the impact of the 1899 depression and the horrors associated with the Russo-Japanese war were realized, groups advocating revolutions commanded little support. Even when the Revolution of 1905 occurred, the Marxist groups did not enjoy any political gains. By the winter (1904 – 05), the accumulated consequences of inept management of the economy and in the prosecution of the Russo-Japanese War reached a critical stage. A group under the leadership of the radical priest Gapon marched on the Winter Palace in St. Petersburg (January 9, 1905) to submit a list of grievances to the Czar; troops fired on the demonstrators and many casualties resulted on this "Bloody Sunday". In response to the massacre, a general strike was called; it was followed by a series of peasant revolts through the spring. During these same months, the Russian armed forces were being defeated by the Japanese and a lack of confidence in the regime became widespread. In June 1905, naval personnel on the battleship *Potemkin* mutinied while the ship was in Odessa. With this startling development, Nicholas II's government lost its nerve. In October 1905, Nicholas II issued the *October Manifesto* which called for the convocation of a Duma, or assembly of state, which would serve as an advisory body to the Czar; extended civil liberties to include freedom of speech, assembly, and press; and announced that Nicholas II would reorganize his government.

The leading revolutionary forces differed in their responses to the manifesto. The *Octobrists* indicated that they were satisfied with the arrangements; the *Constitutional Democrats*, also known as the *Cadets*, demanded a more liberal representative system. The Duma convened in 1906 and, from its outset to the outbreak of the First World War, was paralyzed by its own internal factionalism which was exploited by the Czar's ministers. By 1907 Nicholas II's ministers had recovered the real power of government. Russia experienced a general though fragile economic recovery which was evident by 1909 and lasted until the war.

## 6.2 THE HAPSBURGS IN DECLINE: AUSTRIA-HUNGARY

After the disruptions of the Revolution of 1848 and 1849, the Austrian government had to address a series of major issues with which it found itself confronted:

1) The issue of German nationalism – the *Kleindeutsch* and the *Grossdeutsch* (see Chapter 2);

2) the problems associated with the rise of the national aspirations of the ethnic groups which resided in the Balkans; and

3) the management of an empire which was not integrated because of historic tradition and cultural diversification.

During the 1850s the Hapsburg leadership deferred any attempt to resolve these problems, and in doing so, lost the initiative. To the north, Bismarck was developing the Prussian army in anticipation for the struggle with Austria over the future of Germany; in the Balkans, the Hungarians and Czechs, while smarting from the setbacks of 1849, were agitating for national self-determination or, at the least, for a semi-autonomous state. In 1863 and 1864 Austria became involved with Prussia in a war with Denmark. This war was a prelude for the German Civil War of 1866 between Austria and Prussia; Prussia prevailed. The impact of these developments on the Austrian government necessitated a reappraisal of its national policies. Without doubt the most significant development resulting from this reappraisal was the *Ausgleich* or Compromise, which transformed Austria into the Austro-Hungarian Empire. The Hungarians would have their own assembly, cabinet, and administrative system, and would support and participate in the Imperial army and in the Imperial government. Not only did the *Ausgleich* assimilate the Hungarians and nullify them as a primary opposition group, it also led to a more efficient government.

During the period from 1867 to 1914, Austria-Hungary continued to experience difficulties with the subject nationalities and with adjusting to a new power structure in Central Europe in which Austria-Hungary was admittedly secondary to Germany. At the same time, it enjoyed a cultural revival in which its scholars (Sigmund Freud, Carl Menger, and Heinrich Friedjung), painters (Hans Makart and Adalvert Stiftor), dramatists (Hugo von Hofmannsthal), and writers (Stefan Zweig and Rilke) were renowned throughout the world.

# 6.3 THE BALKAN STATES AND THE DISINTEGRATION OF THE OTTOMAN EMPIRE

During the period from 1848 to 1914 the influence of the Ottoman Empire was eroded steadily because of its own internal structure and system, the ineptitude of its leaders, the lack of cohesion within the empire, the development of nationalist ambitions among many ethnic groups in the region, and the expansionist policies of Austria-Hungary and Russia in the Balkans, and of Great Britain in the eastern Mediterranean.

By 1914 Rumania, Serbia, Bulgaria, and Montenegro had been established as independent states, Austria had annexed Bosnia and Herzegovina, Britain held Cyprus, and Russia had extended its influence over the new Bulgaria.

# CHAPTER 7

# THE NEW IMPERIALISM, 1870 – 1914

## 7.1 ORIGINS, MOTIVES, AND IMPLICATIONS OF THE NEW IMPERIALISM

During the first seven decades of the nineteenth century, the European powers did not pursue active imperial expansion. Internal European development preoccupied the powers; colonies were viewed as liabilities because of the direct costs associated with their administration. However, this attitude to extra-European activity began to change in the 1870s and, within the next twenty years, most of the European states were conducting aggressive imperial policies. This sharp departure from previous policy was caused by economic, political, and cultural factors. By the 1870s the European industrial economies had developed to a level where they required external markets to distribute the products which could not be absorbed within their domestic economies. Further, excess capital was available and foreign investment, while with some risk, appeared to offer the promise of high return. Finally, the need for additional sources of raw materials served as an economic rationale and stimulant for imperialism. In part, these economic considerations arose from the existing political forces of the era and, at the same time, motivated the contemporary political leadership to be sympathetic in their reappraisal of imperialism. Politicians were also influenced by the numerous missionary societies which sought government protection, if not support, in extending Christianity throughout the world; British and French missionary societies were vehement in their anti-slavery position. Further, European statesmen, cognizant of the emergence of a new distribution of power in Europe, were interested in asserting their national power overseas through the acquisition of strategic – and many not so strategic – colonies. Disraeli and Salisbury of England, Thiers and Ferry of France, and later Bismarck of Germany were influenced by yet another factor: the European cultural sentiments of the 1870s and 1880s. The writings of John Seeley, Anatole Leroy-Beaulieu and others suggested that the future status of the powers would be dependant upon the extent and significance of their imperial holdings; these thoughts were later amplified by the social and national Darwinists. Exploration and imperial policies were supported by the public throughout the era; national pride and economic opportunities were the factors upon which this popular support was based.

Unlike colonial policies of earlier centuries, the "New Imperialism" of the 1870s was comprehensive in scope and, as Benjamin Disraeli argued in 1872, a call to "greatness" where a nation was to fulfill its destiny. From Disraeli to Kipling to Churchill, there were few leaders who would differ sharply from this view. On the continent, the New Imperialism was opposed most vigorously by orthodox Marxists; even the revisionist groups such as the *Social Democratic Party* and, during the Boer War, the English *Fabian Society*, supported imperial policies.

# 7.2  THE SCRAMBLE FOR COLONIES

The focus of most of the European imperial activities during the late nineteenth century was Africa. Since the 1850s, Africa had commanded the attention of European explorers such as Richard Burton, Carl Peters, David Livingston, and many others, who were interested in charting the unknown interior of the continent, and, in particular, in locating the headwaters of the Nile. Initially, European interest in these activities was romantic; with John Hanning Speke's discovery of Lake Victoria (1858), Livingston's surveying of the Zambezi, and Stanley's work on the Congo River, Europeans became enraptured with the greatness and novelty of Africa south of the Sahara.

While Disraeli was involved in the intrigue which would result in the British acquisition of the Suez Canal (1875), Britain found itself becoming increasingly involved in establishing itself as an African power. During the 1870s and 1880s Britain was involved in a Zulu War and announced the annexation of the Transvaal, which the Boers regained after their great victory of Majuba Hill (1881) over the British. At about the same time, Belgium established its interest in the Congo; France, in addition to seizing Tunisia, extended its influence into French Equitorial Africa, which was the Ubangui River Basin; and Italy established small colonies in East Africa which would later be extended. During the 1880s Germany became interested in African acquisitions and acquired several African colonies including German East Africa, the Cameroons, Togoland, and German South West Africa. All of these imperial activities heightened tensions among the European powers. Consequently, the *Berlin Conference* (1884 – 85) was convened. The conference resulted in an agreement which specified the following:

# EUROPEAN IMPERIALISM IN AFRICA, 1914

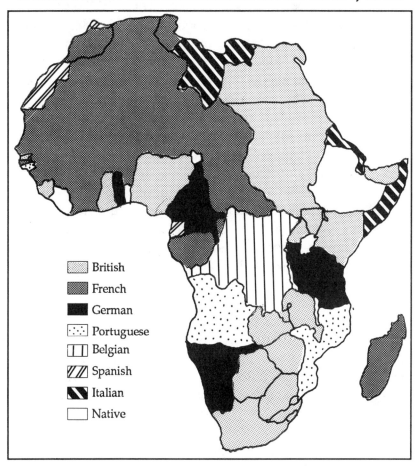

British
French
German
Portuguese
Belgian
Spanish
Italian
Native

1) The Congo would be under the control of Belgium through an International Association;

2) more liberal use of the Niger and Congo rivers; and

3) European powers could acquire African territory through (1) occupation and (2) notifying the other European states of their occupation and claim.

Between 1885 and 1914 the principal European states continued to enhance their positions in Africa. Without doubt, Britain was the most active and successful. From 1885 to 1890 Britain expanded its control over Nigeria, moved north from the Cape of Good Hope, and became further involved in East Africa. By this time Salisbury was the leader of the Conservative Party and, when in office, he fostered imperial expansion. Gladstone was still an anti-imperialist and the leader of the Liberal Party; he found the imperialist forces so formidable that he had to compromise his position on occasion when he was Prime Minister. During the 1880s an Islamic revolution under the *Mahdi*, an Islamic warrior, developed in the Sudan. In 1884 Gladstone sent General Charles Gordon to evacuate Khartoum; Gordon and the city's defenders were slaughtered by the Mahdi's forces in January, 1885. The British found themselves confronted with a continuing native insurrection in the Sudan which was not suppressed effectively until Kitchener's victory at Omdurman in 1898. The French were also quite active during this period; they unified Senegal, the Ivory Coast, and Guinea into French West Africa and extended it to Timbuktu, and moved up the Ubangui toward Lake Chad. While the British had difficulties in the Sudan, the French had to suppress a native insurrection in Madagascar which was prolonged to 1896.

The British movement north of the Cape of Good Hope resulted in a different type of struggle – one that involved Europeans fighting one another rather than a native African force. The *Boers* had a developed settlement in South Africa since the beginning of the nineteenth century. With the discovery of gold (1882) in the Transvaal, many English Cape settlers moved into the region. The Boers, under the leadership of Paul Kruger, restricted the political and economic rights of the British settlers and developed alternative railroads through Mozambique which would lessen the Boer dependency on the

48

Cape colony. Relations between the British and Boers steadily deteriorated; in 1895, the *Jameson Raid*, an ill-conceived action not approved by Britain, failed to result in restoring the status of British citizens. The crisis mounted and, in 1899, the Boer War began; from 1899 to 1903, the British and Boers fought a war which was costly to both sides. Britain prevailed and by 1909, the Transvaal, Orange Free State, Natal, and the Cape of Good Hope were united into the Union of South Africa.

Another area of increased imperialist activity was the Pacific, where the islands appealed to many nations. In 1890, the American naval Captain Alfred Mahan published *The Influence of Sea Power Upon History*; in this book he argued that history demonstrated that those nations which controlled the seas prevailed. During the 1880s and 1890s naval ships required coaling stations. While Britain, the Netherlands, and France demonstrated that they were interested in Pacific islands, the most active states in this region during the last twenty years of the nineteenth century were Germany and the United States. Britain's Pacific interests were motivated primarily in sustaining its control of Australia. The French were interested in Tahiti; after a dispute with France over the Samoan Islands, the islands were split with France, Germany, and the United States. The United States acquired the Philippines in 1898; Germany gained part of New Guinea, and the Marshall, Caroline, and Mariana island chains. The European powers were also interested in the Asian mainland. In 1900, the *Boxer Rebellion* broke in Peking; it was a native reaction against Western influence in China. An international force was organized to break the siege of the Western legations. Most powers agreed with the American *Open Door Policy* which recognized the independence and integrity of China and provided economic access for all the powers. Rivalry over China (Manchuria) was a principal cause for the outbreak of the Russo-Japanese War in 1904.

# CHAPTER 8

# THE AGE OF BISMARCK, 1871 – 1890

## 8.1 THE DEVELOPMENT OF THE GERMAN EMPIRE

During the period from the establishment of the German Empire in January 1871 to his dismissal as Chancellor of Germany in March 1890, Otto von Bismarck dominated European diplomacy and established an integrated political and economic structure for the new German state. Bismarck established a statist system which was reactionary in political philosophy and based upon industrialism, militarism and innovative social legislation. German adaptation during the *Grundjahre* (the founding years of the new industrial order, 1870 – 1875) was staggering; remarkable increases in productivity and the expansion of industrialization took place during the first twenty years of the German Empire's history.

Until the mid-nineteenth century, Germany consisted of numerous independent states which tended to be identified with regional rather than national concerns; to a large degree, this condition reflected the continuing impact of the Peace of Westphalia (1648). With the unification of Germany (see Chapter 2), a German state became a reality but the process of integration of regional economic, social, political, and cultural interests had not yet occurred. Bismarck, with the consent and approval of Wilhelm I, the German Emperor, developed a constitution for the new nation which provided for the following:

1) The Emperor would be the executor of state and, as such, establish the domestic and foreign policies; he was also the commander of the armed forces. The Chancellor (similar to Prime Minister) held office at the discretion of the Emperor.

2) A bicameral legislature was established. It consisted of the *Reichstag*; a lower body which represented the nation (the *Volk*); and the *Bundesrat*, an upper body which represented the various German states. During Bismarck's tenure the Bundesrat identified with reactionary conservative positions and served to check any populism which would be reflected in the Reichstag.

During the 1870s and 1880s Bismarck's domestic policies were directed at the establishment of a united strong German state which would be capable of defending itself from a French war of revenge which would be designed to restore Alsace-Lorraine to France. Laws were enacted which unified the monetary system, established an Imperial Bank and strengthened existing banks, developed universal German civil and criminal codes, and required compulsory military service. All of these measures contributed to the integration of the German state.

The German political system was multi-party. The most significant political parties of the era were (1) the Conservatives, which represented the *Junkers* of Prussia, (2) the Pro-

51

gressives, which unsuccessfully sought to extend democracy through continuing criticism of Bismarck's autocratic procedures; (3) the National Liberals, who represented the German middle class and identified with German nationalism and who provided support for Bismarck's policies; (4) the Center Party (also known as the Catholic Party), which approved Bismarck's policy of centralization and promoted the political concept of Particularism which advocated regional priorities, and (5) the Social Democratic Party (S.P.D.), a Marxist group, which advocated sweeping social legislation, the realization of genuine democracy, and the demilitarization of the German government. Bismarck was unsuccessful in stopping the influence of the Center Party through his anti-Catholic *Kulturkampf* (the May Laws) and in thwarting the growth of the Social Democrats.

In order to develop public support for the government and to minimize the threat from the left, Bismarck instituted a protective tariff, which maintained domestic production, and many social and economic laws which provided social security, regulated child labor, and improved working conditions for all Germans.

## 8.2   EUROPEAN DIPLOMACY

Bismarck's foreign policy was centered on the primary principle of maintaining the diplomatic isolation of France. After a few years of recovery from their defeat in the Franco-Prussian War, the French were regaining their confidence and publicly discussing the feasibility of a war of revenge to regain Alsace-Lorraine. In 1875, the *War-In-Sight-Crisis* occurred between the French and Germans; while war was avoided, the crisis clearly indicated the delicate state of the Franco-German relationship. In the crisis stemming from the Russo-Turkish War (1877 – 78), Bismarck tried to serve as the "Honest Broker" at the Congress of Berlin (see Chapter 5). Russia did not succeed at the conference and, incorrectly, blamed Bismarck for its failure. Early in the next year, a cholera epidemic affected Russian cattle herds and Germany placed an embargo on the importation of Russian beef. The Russians were outraged by the German action and launched an anti-German propaganda campaign in the Russian press. Bismarck, desiring to maintain the peace and a predictable diplomatic environment, concluded a secret defensive treaty with Austria-Hungary in 1879. The *Dual Alliance* was very significant because it was the first "hard" diplomatic alliance of the era. A "hard" alliance involved the specific commitment of military support; traditional or "soft" alliances involved pledges of neutrality or to hold military conversations in the event of a war. The Dual Alliance, which had a five year term and was renewable, directed that one signatory would assist the other in the event that one power was attacked by two or more states.

In 1881, another similar agreement, the *Triple Alliance*, was signed between Germany, Austria-Hungary, and Italy. In the 1880s, relations between Austria-Hungary and Russia became estranged over Balkan issues. Bismarck, fearing a war, intervened and, by 1887, had negotiated the secret *Reinsurance Treaty* with Russia. This was a "hard" defensive alliance with a three year term, renewable. Since these were "defensive" arrangements, Bismarck was confident that through German policy the general European peace would be maintained and the security of Germany ensured through sustaining the diplomatic isolation of France. Bismarck also acted to neutralize the role of Great Britain in European affairs through the implementation of a policy which, in most but not all instances, was supportive of British interests.

In 1888 Wilhelm I died and was succeeded by his son Frederich III who also died within a few months. Friedrich's son, Wilhelm II (1888 – 1918), came to power and soon found himself in conflict with Bismarck. Wilhelm II was intent upon administering the government personally and viewed Bismarck as an archaic personality. Early in 1890 two issues developed which led ultimately to Bismarck's dismissal. First, Bismarck had evolved a scheme for a fabricated attempted *coup* by the Social Democratic Party; his interest was to use this situation to create a national hysteria through which he could restrict the SPD through legal action. Secondly, Bismarck intended to renew the Reinsurance Treaty with Russia to maintain his policy of French diplomatic isolation. Wilhelm II opposed both of these plans; in March 1890, Bismarck, who had used the threat of resignation so skillfully in the past, suggested that he would resign if Wilhelm II would not approve of these actions. Wilhelm II accepted his resignation; in fact, Bismarck was dismissed. The diplomatic developments after 1890 (see Chapter 11) radically altered the alignment of power in Europe. The position of Chancellor of Germany was filled by a series of less talented statesmen including Count von Caprivi (1890 – 94), Prince Hohenlohe (1894 – 1900), Prince Bernhard von Bulow (1900 – 1909), and Chancellor Bethmann-Hollweg.

# CHAPTER 9

# THE MOVEMENT TOWARD DEMOCRACY IN WESTERN EUROPE TO 1914

## 9.1   GREAT BRITAIN

Even after the reform measures of 1867 and 1884 to 1885 (see Chapter 5), the movement toward democratic reforms in Great Britain continued unabated. Unlike other European nations where the focus on democracy was limited to gaining the vote, British reform efforts were much more complex and sophisticated and involved social and economic reforms as well as continuing changes in the political process; participation in the system as well as representation were desired by many. During the 1880s and 1890s new groups emerged which intended to extend the definition of democratic government to embrace new social and economic philosophies of the period. From women's suffrage and the condemnation of imperialism to the redistribution of wealth and the demise of nationalism, these groups represented a broad spectrum of radical and reform ideologies. Among the most significant was the Fabian

Society (1883) which advanced a mode of revisionist Marxism and whose members included Sidney and Beatrice Webb, the Scottish politician Keir Hardie (who later led the Labor Party), George Bernard Shaw, H. G. Wells, the historian C. D. H. Cole, and the young Ramsay MacDonald, who became the first Labor Prime Minister. The Fabians argued for evolutionary political transformation which would result in full political democracy and economic socialism. In 1884, the Social Democratic Federation was formed by H. M. Hyndman. In 1893, Keir Hardie established the *Independent Labor Party* which rapidly became a vocal third party in British politics. The Labor Party attracted trade unionists, socialists, and those who thought that the Conservative and Liberal Parties had no genuine interest in the needs of the general public.

During the early years of the twentieth century both the Conservatives and the Liberals advanced more aggressive social and economic programs. The Conservatives, through the efforts of Arthur James Balfour, promoted the *Education Act of 1902* which they argued would provide enhanced educational opportunities for the working class. In fact, this act was criticized soundly for not providing what it claimed as its purpose. In 1905, the Liberals under Henry Campbell-Bannerman came to power. The government ministries were staffed by such talented leaders as Herbert Asquith, Sir Edward Grey, David Lloyd George, and Winston Churchill. The most significant political reform of this long-lived Liberal government was the *Parliament Act of 1911* which eliminated the powers of the House of Lords and resulted in the House of Commons becoming the unquestioned center of national power:

1) All revenue bills approved by the House of Commons would automatically become law thirty days after being sent to the House of Lords. If the Lords voted favora-

bly, the law would be enacted earlier. The Lords had no veto power.

2) Non-revenue bills which were opposed by the Lords would be enacted if passed by three consecutive sessions of Commons. It was not difficult to transform such measures into revenue bills.

3) The life-span of Parliament was reduced from seven to five years.

The British political climate during this period was rather volatile. Issues relating to trade unions, Ireland, and women's suffrage tended to factionalize British politics. The Liberal Party, which was in power from 1905 to the early 1920s, came to be institutionalized and in the process came to be identified as "the government." To many, the programs advanced by the Conservative and Labor parties provided the basis for debate and decision. The Liberal Party was withering because it lacked clarity of platform and encapsulated the unrealized domestic goals, the ambiguities of bureaucracy, and the horrors of war.

The most recurring and serious problem which Great Britain experienced during the period from 1890 to 1914 was the "Irish Question". Gladstone, in his final ministry, argued unsuccessfully for Irish Home Rule. In Ireland opposition to British rule and the abuses of British power was evident through the program of the *National Land League*, which was established in 1879 by Michael Davitt. This organization stimulated and coordinated Irish opposition to British and Irish landlords. The efforts of the National Land League resulted in support for Irish Home Rule. During the 1880s Charles Stewart Parnell led the Irish delegation to the House of Commons. Parnell, through the support of Gladstone, attained some gains for the Irish such as the *Land Reform Act* and the *Arrears Act*. In 1890 Parnell became involved in a divorce case and the scandal ruined his career; he died the next year. In 1893 Gladstone devised the Irish Home Rule bill which was passed by the House of Commons but rejected by the House of Lords. The Irish situation became more complicated when the Protestant counties of the north started to enjoy remarkable economic growth from the mid-1890s; they were adamant in their rejection of all measures of Irish Home Rule. In 1914, an Irish Home Rule Act was passed by both the Commons and the Lords but the Protestants refused to accept it; implementation was deferred until after the war.

## 9.2   THE THIRD FRENCH REPUBLIC

In the fall of 1870, Napoleon III's Second Empire collapsed when it was defeated by the Prussian armies. Napoleon III and his principal aides were captured; later, he abdicated and fled to England. A National Assembly (1871 – 75) was created and Adolphe Thiers was recognized as its chief executive. At the same time, a more radical political entity, the *Paris Commune* (1870 – 71), came into existence and exercised extraordinary power during the siege of Paris. After the siege and the peace agreement with Prussia, the Paris Commune refused to recognize the authority of the National Assembly. Led by radical Marxists, anarchists, and republicans, the Paris Commune repudiated the conservative and monarchist leadership of the National Assembly; from March to May 1871, the Paris Commune fought a bloody struggle with the troops of the National Assembly. Thousands died and when Paris surrendered, there were thousands of executions – accepted estimates place the number of executions at 20,000 during the first week after Paris fell on May 28, 1871. It was within this historic framework that France began a program of recovery which led to the formulation of the Third French Republic in 1875. The National Assembly sought to (1) put the French political house in order, (2) establish a new constitutional government, (3) pay off an imposed indemnity and, in doing so, remove German troops from French territory, and (4) restore the honor and glory of France. In 1875 a Constitution was adopted which provided for a republican government with a president (with little power), a Senate, and a Chamber of Deputies, which was the center of political power. The politicians and factions which led France during the 1870s and 1880s had to address the dominant forces which served as the dynamic elements of French politics. These forces included the overwhelming influence of the French *bourgeoisie* (middle class), which was intent upon establishing and sustaining a French republican government; the mounting hostility between the Catholic Church and the French government (anti-clericalism was frequently manifested in the proceedings of the Chamber of Deputies); the unpredictability which accompanied multi-party politics; and, finally, the extreme nationalism which gripped France during these decades and which resulted in continuing calls for a war of revenge against Germany in order to regain Alsace-Lorraine.

During the early years of the Republic, Leon Gambetta (1838 – 1882) led the republicans. Beginning in the 1880s the Third French Republic was challenged by a series of crises which threatened the continuity of the Republic. *The Boulanger Crisis* (1887 – 1889), the *Panama Scandal* (1894), and the *Dreyfus Affair* (1894 – 1906) were serious domestic problems; in all of these developments, the challenge to republicanism came from the right. The sustenance of republicanism through this time of troubles came primarily from (1) the able leadership of the republican government, and (2) the continuing commitment of the *bourgeoisie* to republicanism. Since the founding of the Third Republic, monarchists and conservatives were interested in overthrowing the regime; however, until the appointment of General Georges Boulanger (1837 – 1891) as

59

Minister of War in 1886, there was no one to lead the anti-republican cause. Boulanger won over the army by improving the basic conditions of military life. His public popularity was high in 1888 and his supporters urged him to conduct a *coup*; he delayed and by the spring of 1889, the republicans had mounted a case against Boulanger. He was directed to appear to respond to charges of conspiracy; Boulanger broke, fled to Belgium, and committed suicide in 1891. The Boulanger crisis resulted in renewed confidence in the republic; but what popular gains it made were unravelled in 1892 with the Panama Scandal. The French had been involved with the engineering and the raising of capital for the Panama Canal since the 1870s. Early in the 1890s the promoters of the project resorted to the bribery of government officials and of certain members of the press who had access to information which indicated that the work on the canal was not proceeding as had been announced. In 1892 the scandal broke and for months the public indicated that it thought that the entire French government was corrupt. However, by 1893, elections to the Chamber of Deputies resulted in the socialists making notable gains; the monarchists did not attract much public support.

Without a doubt, the most serious threat to the republic came through the *Dreyfus Affair*. In 1894 Captain Alfred Dreyfus was assigned to the French General Staff; a scandal broke when it was revealed that classified information had been provided to German spies. Dreyfus, a Jew, was charged, tried, and convicted. Later, it was determined that the actual spy was Commandant Marie Charles Esterhazy; however, he was acquitted in order to save the pride and reputation of the army. The monarchists used this incident to criticize republicanism; the republicans countered when Emile Zola took up Dreyfus's cause when he wrote an open letter entitled *J'accuse*, which condemned the General Staff's actions and pronounced Dreyfus's innocence. Leftists supported the Republic and, in

1906, the case was closed when Dreyfus was declared innocent and returned to the ranks. Rather than lead to the collapse of the republic, the Dreyfus Affair demonstrated the intensity of anti-Semitism in French society, the level of corruption in the French army, and the willingness of the Catholic Church and the monarchists to join in a conspiracy against an innocent man. The republicans launched an anti-clerical campaign which included the *Association Act* (1901) and the separation of church and state (1905).

From 1905 to 1914 the socialists under Jean Juares gained seats in the Chamber of Deputies. The Third French Republic endured the crises which confronted it and, in 1914, enjoyed the support of the vast majority of French citizens.

## 9.3 THE LESSER STATES OF WESTERN, NORTHERN, AND SOUTHERN EUROPE

In the Low Countries during the decades prior to 1914 there were differing approaches to extending democracy. An appreciation of democracy was evident in Belgium under the leadership of Leopold I (1865 – 1909) and Albert I (1909 – 1934); during their reigns the franchise was extended, social and economic reforms were introduced, and equity was the basis of the settlement between Flemish and French speaking Belgians. To the north, the Netherlands was slow to adopt democracy. By 1896, only 14% of the Dutch had the vote and it would not be until 1917 that universal manhood suffrage would be enacted.

Denmark experienced a struggle between the old guard represented by Christian IX (1863 – 1906), who opposed parliamentary government, and the Social Democrats who advocated democratic principles. The Danish Constitution of 1915 provided a basic democratic political system. Sweden, after a decade of debilitating debate, recognized the independence of Norway in 1905; Norway moved quickly toward democracy, granting women full suffrage in 1913. Sweden, under Gustavus V (1907 – 1950), pronounced a comprehensive democratic system in 1909.

In southern Europe advocates of democracy did not meet with any substantive success prior to 1914, where monarchist establishments were preoccupied with survival. Spain was a parliamentary monarchy until 1931; Portugal had a very unstable Republican government from 1910 to 1926; Italy was a parliamentary monarchy until after World War II. While an occasional reform was promulgated, there was no intent to move toward full democracy.

# CHAPTER 10

# EUROPEAN CULTURAL DEVELOPMENTS, 1848 – 1914

The great political and economic changes of this period were accompanied by cultural achievements which included the development of a literate citizenry and substantive innovations in science, literature, art, music and other areas of intellectual activity. In large part, these developments occurred as a reaction against the mechanistic sterility of the scientism and positivism of the age; however, some of the initial achievements, such as Darwin's theories of evolution and natural selection, resulted in extending the exaggerated claims of scientism. From Charles Darwin, Richard Wagner, Friedrich Nietzsche, and Sigmund Freud to Claude Monet, Richard Strauss, Igor Stravinsky, Oscar Wilde, Thomas Mann, and James Joyce, intelligent Europeans of the era pursued many differing, and at times opposing, approaches in their quest for truth and understanding. Many philosophers were critical of the movement toward democracy which they identified with mass culture and political ineptitude. Artists attempted to escape their plight through moving into symbolism with their pen or brush; there, they were free to express their fantasies of hope and despair.

## 10.1  DARWIN, WAGNER, FREUD, AND THE EMERGENCE OF A NEW TRADITION

In 1859, Charles Darwin's (1807 – 1882) *The Origins of the Species* was published; it argued the theory of evolution which had been discussed for more than a generation in Europe. Darwin's contributions to the advocacy of this theory were based (1) on the data which he provided to demonstrate the theory, and (2) in the formulation of a well structured and argued defense of the theory of natural selection (survival of the fittest). The reaction to *The Origins of the Species* was diverse, thorough, and enduring; some discussants were concerned with the implication of the theory on religion, while others were interested in applying aspects of the theory to the understanding of contemporary social problems. Within the Darwinian camp, factions emerged which supported or rejected one or more components of the theory. Samuel Butler and George Bernard Shaw accepted evolution but rejected natural selection; Thomas Huxley was Darwin's most consistent and loyal supporter. Herbert Spencer (1820 – 1903) developed a Social Darwinism which enjoyed extensive acceptance in both scholarly and general circles. One of the obvious consequences of Darwin's theory was that it necessitated a reevaluation of all of the issues relating to man's place in the cosmos. The doctrine of creation was challenged and thus the authenticity of prevailing religion was endangered.

In classical music, the erratic Richard Wagner (1813 – 1883) reflected the incongruities and the harshness of the new age. Wagner developed and imposed an aestheticism that had one fundamental element – it demanded absolute artistic integrity. Wagner shifted styles several times during his career; his

*Ring* cycle was centered on German epics and advanced numerous fantasies about the history of the German people.

Sigmund Freud (1856 – 1939) established a new approach to understanding human behavior which was known as psychoanalysis. Freud accepted the impressionist interpretation that reality was not material; rather it was based on moods, concepts, and feelings which shift. In Vienna, Freud developed his concepts that the unconscious was shaped during the formative years, that sexuality was a dominant lifeforce, and that free will may not exist. Freud argued his theories in a formidable body of literature which included the *Origins of Psychoanalysis* and *Civilization and Its Discontents*. The establishment rejected his unorthodox views as threats to religion.

In science itself, new developments challenged the certainty and security of the old science. Max Planck's *Quantum Physics*, Albert Einstein's *Theory of Relativity*, and the impact of the *Michelson-Morley Experiment* (1887; regarding the measurement of speed; conducted in the United States) led to a new generation of scientists re-examining many of the assumptions of the past.

## 10.2 IMPRESSIONISM AND SYMBOLISM: FORCES OF THE NEW ART

The turbulence within European cultural life during the fifty years prior to the outbreak of the First World War can be seen most evidently in new attitudes which emerged in art and literature. Not only did the intellectuals find themselves looking for a new intellectual synthesis through which to offer new vision and hope, but also they were liberated from the limitations which had been imposed on their predecessors through a technological breakthrough. The development of photography resulted in artists no longer being required to produce actual representations. Painters were now free to pursue the dictates of their imaginations. *Impressionism* developed in France during the 1870s; Monet, Manet, Renoir, and others pioneered the new art. Impressionism soon gave way to *Post-Impressionism* and later *Expressionism*. At the turn of the century, more radical artistic forms such as *Symbolism* and *Cubism* enjoyed notoriety if not general acceptance.

Literature was transformed through the writings of such innovators as Oscar Wilde (*The Picture of Dorian Gray*), Thomas Mann (*Death in Venice*), and the young James Joyce (prior to 1914, *Portrait of the Artist as a Young Man* and *Dubliners*). These writers were interested in discussing the themes which had great personal value and meaning; Joyce will emerge as the most seminal stylist of the twentieth century.

# CHAPTER 11

# INTERNATIONAL POLITICS AND THE COMING OF THE WAR, 1890 – 1914

During the generation prior to the outbreak of the First World War in the summer of 1914, conflicts and strained relations among the great powers increased in frequency and intensity. There can be no question that the primary factors which contributed to this situation were the heightened nationalism and the cultural materialism of the period.

## 11.1 THE POLARIZATION OF EUROPE

In March 1890 Bismarck was dismissed as Chancellor of Germany by the immature, impetuous, and inexperienced Kaiser Wilhelm II. The particular issues which led to Bismarck's fall included the renewal of the *Reinsurance Treaty* (1887) with Russia and Bismarck's scheme to weaken the role of the Social Democratic Party (SPD) within German politics. With Bismarck's dismissal, the continuing dominance of the German agenda over European affairs was questionable. The intricate alliance system which Bismarck had constructed was directed at maintaining the diplomatic isolation of France.

Germany failed to renew the Reinsurance Treaty with Russia and consequently Russia looked elsewhere to eliminate its own perceived isolation. In 1891 secret negotiations were entered into by the French and Russians. By 1894 these deliberations resulted in the *Dual Entente* which was a comprehensive military alliance. This agreement was sustained through 1917 and allowed France to pursue a more assertive foreign policy. From the Russian perspective, the fears of isolation and of the development of an anti-Russian combination were abated. Within four years of Bismarck's dismissal, the essential imperative of German foreign policy in the late nineteenth century – the diplomatic isolation of France – was no longer a reality.

In 1895 a new Conservative government came to power in Great Britain. Led by Lord Salisbury, who served as Prime Minister and Foreign Secretary, this government included a wide range of talented statesmen including Joseph Chamberlain, John Morley, Lord Landsdowne, and the young Arthur James Balfour. The Salisbury government was interested in terminating the long-standing policy of "Splendid Isolationism" which had prevailed as Britain's response to European alliances. Salisbury came to argue that the new realities of world politics and economics deemed it advisable for Britain to ally itself with a major power. While coming under general European criticism for its role in the Boer War (1899 – 1902) in South Africa, British representatives approached Berlin in an attempt to develop an Anglo-German alliance. Germany declined the British advances because (1) the Germans were sympathetic to the Boers, (2) the Germans questioned the ability of the British army, (3) they believed that the British would never be able to reach an accommodation with the French or Russians, and (4) Wilhelm II was involved in a major naval building program – this effort would be jeopardized if the Germans were allied to the world's greatest naval power, Britain.

Consequently, Britain pursued diplomatic opportunities which resulted in the *Anglo-Japanese Alliance* (1902), the *Entente Cordiale* or *Anglo-French Entente* (1904), and the Anglo-Russian Entente (1907).

The *Anglo-Japanese Alliance* of 1902 resulted in the two powers agreeing to adopt a position of benevolent neutrality in the event that the other member state was involved in war; this arrangement was sustained through the First World War.

The *Entente Cordiale* (1904), which is also known as the *Dual Entente* or the *Anglo-French Entente*, was a settlement of long-standing colonial disputes between Britain and France over North African territories. It was agreed that northeast Africa (Egypt and the Anglo-Egyptian Sudan) would be a British sphere of influence and that northwest Africa (Morocco) would be a French sphere of influence. This was a colonial settlement, not a formal alliance; neither power pledged support in the event of war. However, the *Entente Cordiale* was of critical significance because it drew Britain into the French oriented diplomatic camp.

While Anglo-French relations improved during 1904 to 1905, the historically tense Anglo-Russian relationship was aggravated further through the Russo-Japanese War (1904 – 05). The *Dogger Bank Incident* resulted in a crisis between these powers when Russian naval ships fired on and sunk several British fishing boats in the North Sea. Britain, which earlier had adopted a sympathetic posture toward Japan, responded by deploying the Home Fleet and curtailing the activities of the Russian fleet. The crisis was resolved when Russia agreed to apologize for the incident and to pay compensation. In 1905 a Liberal government came to power in Britain, and Russia was absorbed in its own revolution which liberalized, at least temporarily, the autocratic regime. Negotiations between these powers were initiated and were facilitated by the French; in 1907 Britain and Russia reached a settlement on their outstanding colonial disputes. They agreed on three points:

1) Persia would be divided into three zones: a northern sector under Russian influence, a southern sector under British control, and a central zone which could be mutually exploited;

2) Afghanistan was recognized as a British sphere of influence;

3) Tibet was recognized as part of China and, as such, was to be free from foreign intervention.

By 1907 France, Britain, and Russia had formed a *Triple Entente* which effectively balanced the Triple Alliance. While Britain was not formally committed to an alliance system, Sir Edward Grey, British Foreign Minister from 1905, supported secret conversations between British and French military representatives. Thus, in terms of military power and economics, Germany became isolated by 1907.

## 11.2   THE RISE OF MILITARISM

During the period after 1890 Europeans began to view the use of military power as not only feasible but also as desirable to bring about a resolution to the increasingly hostile political conditions in Europe. The apparent inability of diplomats to develop lasting settlements supported the further development of this perception. The notion that a major European war was inevitable became acceptable to many.

Within the structure of the European states, militarists enjoyed increased credibility and support. The General Staffs became preoccupied with planning for the anticipated struggle and their plans affected national foreign policies. The Germans, under the influence of General Count Alfred von Schlieffen, developed the *Schlieffen Plan* by 1905. It was predicated on the assumption that Germany would have to conduct a two front war with France and Russia. It specified that France must be defeated quickly through the use of enveloping tactics which involved the use of German armies of about 1,500,000 men. After victory in the west, Germany would then look to the east to defeat the Russians, who would be slow to mobilize. The French developed the infamous *Plan XVII*, which was approved by Marshall Joseph Joffre. The French thought that the German attack would be concentrated in the region of Alsace-Lorraine and that the French forces should be massed in that area; the *élan* of the French soldiery would result in a victory.

## 11.3  THE ARMS RACE

This wave of nationalistic militarism also manifested itself through a continuing arms race which resulted in several threats to the balance of power because of revolutionary technological developments. Field weapons such as mortars and cannons were improved sharply in range, accuracy, and firepower; the machine gun was perfected and produced in quantity. New weapons such as the submarine and airplanes were recognized as having the capacity to be strategic armaments.

In naval weaponry the rivalry between the British and the Germans over capital ships not only exacerbated the deteriorating relationship between the two powers, but also led to restrictions on the national domestic expenditures during peacetime in order to pay for the increasingly costly battleships and cruisers. In 1912, the British-sponsored *Haldane Mission* was sent to Berlin to negotiate an agreement; the Germans were suspicious and distrustful of the British and were not receptive to any proposal.

## 11.4  IMPERIALISM AS A SOURCE OF CONFLICT

During the late nineteenth century the economically motivated "New Imperialism" resulted in further aggravating the relations among the European powers. The struggle for increased world market share, the need for raw materials, and the availability of capital for overseas investment resulted in enhancing the rivalry among the European nations and, on several occasions, in causing crises to develop. The *Fashoda Crisis* (1898 – 99), the *Moroccan Crisis* (1905 – 06), the *Balkan Crisis* (1908), and the *Agadir Crisis* (1911) demonstrated the impact of imperialism in heightening tensions among European states and in creating an environment in which conflict became more acceptable.

The Fashoda Crisis developed between France and Britain when the French, under the influence of Foreign Minister Theophile Delcasse, ordered Commandant Marchant and a small number of French troops to march across Africa and establish a French "presence" near the headwaters of the Nile. Marchant arrived in Fashoda (now Kodok) in 1898; Fashoda was located on the White Nile, south of Khartoum in the Anglo-Egyptian Sudan. A British army under General Herbert Kitchener, having defeated a native rebel army in the battle of Omdurman, advanced to Khartoum where he learned of the French force at Fashoda. Kitchener marched on Fashoda and a major crisis ensued for months. In the end, the French withdrew and recognized the position of the British in the Anglo-Egyptian Sudan; however, for several months there were serious consideration given to a major war over this colonial issue.

The Moroccan Crisis (1905 – 06) developed when Wilhelm II of Germany travelled to Tangier (March 1905) where he made a speech in support of the independence of Morocco; this position was at odds with that agreed to by the British and the French in the *Entente Cordiale*. Initially, the German position prevailed because of lack of organization within the Franco-Russian alliance; however, in 1906, at the *Algerciras Conference*, the German effort was thwarted and the French secured their position in Morocco. Russia, Britain, and even Italy, supported the French on every important issue. German diplomatic isolation – save for the Austrians – became increasingly evident.

The Balkan Crisis of 1908 involved an example of European imperialist rivalry within Europe. Since the Congress of Berlin in 1878, the Austro-Hungarian Empire had administered the Balkan territories of Bosnia and Herzegovina. Austrian influence in this area was opposed by Russia which considered the region as a natural area of Russian influence. Specifically, the Russians hoped to capitalize upon the collapse of the Ottoman Turkish Empire and to gain access to the Mediterranean Sea. In 1908 the decadent Ottoman Empire was experiencing domestic discord which attracted the attention of both the Austrians and the Russians. These two powers agreed that Austria would annex Bosnia and Herzegovina and that Russia would be granted access to the Straits and thus the Mediterranean. Great Britain intervened and demanded that there be no change in the status quo *vis-a-vis* the Straits. Russia backed down from a confrontation but Austria proceeded to annex Bosnia and Herzegovina. The annexation was condemned by the Pan-Slavists who looked to Russia for assistance; a crisis developed and it appeared that war between Austria and Russia was likely. However, the Russians disengaged from the crisis because of their lack of preparedness for a major struggle and because there were clear indications that Germany would support Austria. The Balkan Crisis was another example of the nature of European rivalries and the rather rapid recourse to sabre-rattling on the part of great powers. Further, it demonstrated that the fundamental regional problem – the developing nationalism among the diverse peoples of the Balkans – was not addressed.

The Agadir Crisis (1911) broke when France announced that its troops would be sent to several Moroccan towns to restore order. Germany, fearing French annexation of all of Morocco, responded by sending the *Panther*, a German naval ship, to Agadir. After exchanging threats for several weeks, the French and Germans agreed to recognize Morocco as a French protectorate and to transfer two sections of the French Congo to Germany.

## 11.5 DIPLOMATIC CRISIS OF THE SUMMER, 1914

During the late nineteenth and early twentieth centuries the Ottoman Empire was in a state of collapse. At the same time, Austria and Russia were interested in extending their influence in the region. Further, nationalism among the ethnic groups in the Balkans was rapidly developing. In addition to the Balkan Crisis of 1908 which was mentioned above, the region was involved in the *Italian-Turkish War* (1911) and the *Inter-Balkan Wars* of 1912 and 1913.

On June 28, 1914, Archduke Franz Ferdinand, heir to the Austro-Hungarian throne, and his wife were assassinated while on a state visit to Sarajevo, the capital of Bosnia. Their assassin was a radical Serb, Gavrilo Princip, who opposed Franz Ferdinand's plan to integrate the Slavs more fully into the government. The assassination resulted in a crisis between Austria-Hungary and Serbia. Austria, determined to respond with force as a great power, dispatched a representative, Count Hoyos, to Germany to determine the level of German support in the event of an expanded conflict. The *Hoyos Mission* resulted in the *Blank Cheque* of July 5, 1914 in which Wilhelm II pledged to militarily support Austria. Serbia was accused of serving as a refuge for radical anti-Austrian groups such as the "Black Hand." On July 23rd the Austrian Foreign Minister, Count Berchtold, sent an ultimatum to Serbia. This ten point document was drafted purposely for rejection. On July 25th Serbia responded that, while it was sympathetic with the Austrians on their loss, it must reject the terms of the ultimatum.

Realizing the seriousness of the crisis, the German Chancellor Bethmann–Hollweg and the British Foreign Secretary, Sir Edward Grey, attempted to mediate the conflict; it was too late. The Austrian, French, and Russian foreign offices pursued myopic interests and the first general European war since the Napoleonic era developed. On July 28th Austria declared war on Serbia and, by August 4th, the major powers (with the exception of Italy) were at war. Britain, France, and Russia (*The Allies*) were at war with Germany and Austria-Hungary (*The Central Powers*); later, other nations would join one of the two camps.

The initial military actions did not proceed as planned. The German Schlieffen Plan failed to succeed in the West as a result of German tactical adjustments and the French and British resistance in the *First Battle of the Marne* (September, 1914). The war of movement in the West, which was critical to the success of German strategy, was transformed into a war of trenches. In the East, the Germans scored significant victories over the numerically superior Russians, at the battles of *Tannenberg* and *Masurian Lakes* (August – September 1914).

# CHAPTER 12

# CONCLUSION

Between 1848 and 1914 Europeans experienced revolutionary changes in their culture. These alterations were based on a new sense of reality, and values in which materialism, and the notion of human progress were manifested in the pragmatism of the era. Nationalism, science and technology, and the rapid expansion of the population were primary factors which contributed to these changes and to the further expansion of European culture throughout the world. The growth in the European standard of living was uneven. Western Europe developed most comprehensively; Central Europe – especially German urban centers – witnessed remarkable growth during the last decades of the period; and Southern and Eastern Europe lagged behind and, by 1914, the standard of living had not dramatically improved from that of the earlier century. Reaction to these changes varied from the development of Marxism, anarchism, and trade unionism in response to the adverse consequences of capitalism and industrialism, to the emergence of Impressionism, Expressionism, and Symbolism in reaction to the perceived intellectual sterility of mechanistic positivism. Nineteenth century Europe, which was identified with hope, progress, and rationality, gave way to the uncertainty, violence, and irrationality of the twentieth century. Politically, economically, and culturally, Europe between 1848 and 1914 continued the process of accelerated change which had been initiated in the previous century with revolutionary developments in production, and in the fundamental concepts about the relationships of man and the state and of man and the economy.

# The High School Tutors®

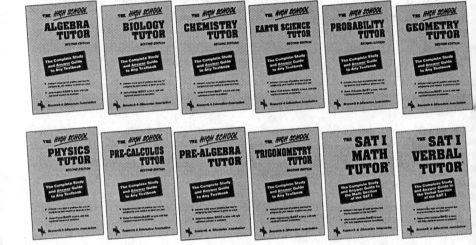

The **HIGH SCHOOL TUTOR** series is based on the same principle as the more comprehensive **PROBLEM SOLVERS**, but is specifically designed to meet the needs of high school students. REA has revised all the books in this series to include expanded review sections and new material. This makes the books even more effective in helping students to cope with these difficult high school subjects.

*If you would like more information about any of these books,*
*complete the coupon below and return it to us or go to your local bookstore.*